Animales del zoológico / Zoo Animals

PINGÜINOS / PENGUINS AT THE ZOO

By Finn Ward
Traducido por Ana María García

Gareth Stevens
PUBLISHING

Please visit our website, www.garethstevens.com. For a free color catalog of all our high-quality books, call toll free 1-800-542-2595 or fax 1-877-542-2596.

Library of Congress Cataloging-in-Publication Data

Ward, Finn.
Penguins at the zoo = Pingüinos / Finn Ward.
pages cm. — (Zoo animals = Animales del zoológico)
Parallel title: Animales del zoológico.
In English and Spanish.
Includes index.
ISBN 978-1-4824-3235-0 (library binding)
1. Penguins—Juvenile literature. 2. Zoo animals—Juvenile literature. I. Title.
QL696.S473W37 2016
598.47—dc23

First Edition

Published in 2016 by
Gareth Stevens Publishing
111 East 14th Street, Suite 349
New York, NY 10003

Editor: Ryan Nagelhout
Designer: Katelyn E. Reynolds

Photo credits: Cover, p. 1 Ellen van Bodegom/Moment/Getty Images; p. 5 YOSHIKAZU TSUNO/AFP/Getty Images; p. 7 Saichon Onnim/Shutterstock.com; pp. 9, 24 (wings) S.Cooper Digital/Shutterstock.com; p. 11 Tshooter/Shutterstock.com; p. 13 TOMO/Shutterstock.com; p. 15 Anton_Ivanov/Shutterstock.com; p. 17 Oli Scarff/Getty Images; p. 19 JUSTIN TALLIS/AFP/Getty Images; pp. 21, 24 (chicks) Volodymyr Goinyk/Shutterstock.com; p. 23 Volt Collection/Shutterstock.com.

Printed in the United States of America

CPSIA compliance information: Batch #CS15GS: For further information contact Gareth Stevens, New York, New York at 1-800-542-2595.

Contenido

Contents

Los pingüinos son animales graciosos que puedes ver en el zoológico.

Penguins are fun animals to see at the zoo.

Son aves.
Pero no pueden volar.

They are birds.
They can't fly.

¡Usan las alas
para nadar!

They use their wings
to swim!

Los pingüinos nadan muy rápido.

Penguins swim very fast.

Les encanta el agua.

They love the water.

Les encanta el frío.

They love the cold.

En los zoológicos
cuidan a los pingüinos.

Zoos take care
of penguins.

Les dan de comer
mucho pescado.

They feed them
lots of fish.

Las crías de pingüino
se llaman polluelos.

Penguin babies
are called chicks.

¡Los polluelos están cubiertos de pelusa!

Chicks are very fuzzy!

Palabras que debes aprender/ Words to Know

(los) polluelos/
chicks

(las) alas/
wings

Índice/Index